Turtle Tears

By J. Suthern Hicks

A Play in Two Acts

Cover Design: Tatiana Minina
A Shophar So Good Book: www.shopharsogood.com

ISBN: 0-9970778-3-2
ISBN-13: 978-0-9970778-3-4

PRODUCTION OVERVIEW

Cast Size
4f, 2m

Duration
120 minutes with intermission (2 hours)

Subgenre
Southern, Comedy-Drama, Older Female Leads, Character-Driven

Target Audience
Appropriate for all audiences

Additional Information
Two cantankerous women fight for peace and independence in their twilight years. Only two things stand in their way, their daughters. Nellie wants nothing more than to live out her days in a house trailer in the desert, but her daughter Margie wants to sell the land while the offers are still hot. Nellie's sister-in-law, Iris, has no home and must rely on the kindness of others, but she has burned all of her bridges. Will she be able to mend the past hurts between she and her daughter Bethany, or will they part ways for once and for all? Set in rural Arizona, where the only things pricklier than the cactus are the wit and drama.

CONSIDERATIONS

Performing Groups
College Theatre, Community Theatre,
Dinner Theatre, Professional Theatre, Shoestring Budget,
Blackbox, Second Stage, Church/Religious Groups

LICENSE DETAILS

Minimum Fee: $50 per performance
Contact: HumbleEntertainment@yahoo.com

PRODUCTION DETAILS

Time Period: Before Cell Phones
Duration: 120 minutes with intermission (2 hours)
Setting: Screened-in-porch of a mobile home
Additional Features: One intermission
Features: Partial front façade of a mobile home
Note: With clever staging, rabbits never need to be seen

For these amazing women:
Azora Laney
Peggy Angeline
Bette Rae
Peggy Cozzi

CAST

In Order of Appearance

NELLIE
IRIS
BETHANY
MARGIE
JIMMY
SAM

CONTENTS

The action throughout takes place on the screened-in porch
of a house trailer. The trailer rests on five acres of
southeastern Arizona desert.

TIME: Before Cell Phones

ACT I
Early August.

ACT II
Six Weeks Later.

The first performance of Turtle Tears was given at the Taber Theatre, Los Angeles, on September 8, 1995, by the Toluca Lake Players. It was Directed by Allison Bergman, and produced by Jean Sportelli. The cast was as follows:

Nellie	Peggy Cozzi
Iris	Bette Rae
Bethany	Dorothy A. Gallagher
Margie	Kathleen Jean Klein
Jimmy	Joe Camareno
Sam	J. Suthern Hicks

Note: The character names of Nellie and Iris have been changed since the original production in 1995. While certain aspects of this work are loosely based on actual events, this is primarily a work of fiction. Names, characters, businesses, places, events, locales, and incidents are either the products of the author's imagination or used in a fictitious manner. Any resemblance to actual persons, living or dead, is purely coincidental.

ACT I

SCENE I

(The curtain opens to reveal a large screened-in-porch. Green Astroturf covers the floor. Upstage left a patio door opens to yard. Upstage center several steps lead to the front door which opens to a mobile home. There are a few too many potted plants scattered around. An old metal mesh patio table and three colorful, but worn, lawn chairs sit center stage. A partially disassembled shotgun rests on the far edge of the table. Several more lawn chairs are stacked against the trailer. Two small, wood, handcrafted tables support an odd assortment of knickknacks. A wobbly wooden rabbit hutch sits along the downstage imaginary wall. Several fans blow hot air around the porch.)

(The house trailer door opens. Iris, a short woman of seventy-eight, enters carrying a salad bowl. Her skin is weathered and free of make-up. Her hair is short and thin. She is wearing shorts that are much too tight for a woman of her age and physique. Her shirt is sleeveless. After folding up a lawn chair and placing it against the trailer, she opens the rabbit hutch door and dumps the bowl. She exits. Moments later, Nellie, a robust woman of eighty-two, enters with a bottle of water. She is wearing a light floppy dress which covers her entire body, except the arms. Nellie opens the rabbit cage and fills a water bottle. After securing the cage door, she places the empty bottle on table. After looking around, she shakes her head disagreeably, retrieves the chair that Iris only moments earlier put away—placing it back where it was originally. She then turns on a fan, picks up water bottle, and exits back into house. After a few beats, the door opens again. Iris enters with a cereal bowl, banana, and carton of milk. She places her breakfast on table and sits to eat. Nellie reenters, holding a newspaper. She sits next to Iris.)

IRIS: Did you water the rabbits?

NELLIE: They were bone dry.

IRIS: Gets awful hot out here on the porch.

NELLIE: Sucks the water right up, the heat does.

IRIS: Should've got another water bottle while we
          were in town.

NELLIE: Oh, the rabbits will be just fine.

IRIS: (*after a short pause, looking at the empty
          chair*). Not much room on this porch for a third
          chair to be sittin' empty.

NELLIE: Oh, I don't think we'll be needing the extra room.

IRIS: Bethany's comin' over from California day after tomorrow.

NELLIE: That'll be nice. I haven't seen Beth since Vern's funeral. Vern always liked that daughter of yours. (*Notices half eaten banana.*) You gonna eat...

IRIS: (*pushes banana towards Nellie*). There's more bananas on top of the fridge.

NELLIE: This'll be just fine, thanks. Is Bethany flying or driving?

IRIS: (*picks up shotgun to prepare it for cleaning*). Said she was goin' to bring her husband's truck.

NELLIE Watch where you point that thing.

IRIS: Said she wanted to visit with me. But I have a feelin' she and Dominick are goin' to ask me to come live with them. She's the only one of my kids that cares about my welfare.

NELLIE: She's a long tall drink of water she is. Poor thing had a rough start in life though. I don't think she ever got over what her step-father did to her. I don't imagine anyone could get over something like that.

IRIS: (*unaware that she is pointing gun at Nellie*). I thought I told you never to bring that up again!

NELLIE: (*pushing barrel of gun away*). Sorry.

IRIS: (*putting an end to the discussion*). Talkin' of

stuff you know nothin' about!

NELLIE: (*quietly opens newspaper*). Wal-Mart stock split again. How much of that did you buy?

IRIS: Three-thousand, I believe.

NELLIE: Three-thousand? Not bad, not bad indeed. Nabisco is down a smidge.

IRIS: Stay away from those junk food companies! The government is givin' away all the snack food.

NELLIE: Why they're not doing any such thing. They can't just give it away.

IRIS: I've been hearin' about all those free cookies on the commercials.

NELLIE: *Fat* free, Iris. They're *fat* free.

IRIS: Speakin' of fat, have you taken your blood pressure pills?

NELLIE: They're for my heart. They have nothing to do with my weight! (*A bird chirps*). Shh, you hear that?

IRIS: Cactus Wren. She's callin' for her man. Spotted him dead in the garden yesterday. Just as well— eatin' up all my seedlings. (*Looks down barrel of gun*). Beat himself to death against the chicken wire tryin' to get out, I 'spose. (*She sets down gun and picks up cereal bowl as she heads towards trailer*).

NELLIE: Chicken wire? The last thing that poor bird saw was your sadistic grin behind the barrel of that shotgun! Don't forget the milk. Milk is liable to

4

spoil out here like this. (*Iris grabs milk and banana peel*). You might want to put the milk on the cereal while you're in the kitchen instead of bringing the whole carton out with you.

IRIS: (*exits into trailer, yells from offstage*). Wouldn't that be a great'? But Shredded Wheat don't last that long. They can engineer an apple to last for months, but they can't figure a way to keep my Shredded Wheat from gettin' soggy after just a few minutes.

NELLIE: Just the same, it might be healthier to leave the milk in the fridge. There's that salmonella stuff going around.

IRIS: I'll take my chances. Soggy Shredded Wheat is probably worse.

NELLIE: Would you bring some magazines on your way back.

IRIS: (*returns with magazines before Nellie finishes asking.*) These here?

NELLIE: Yes, those there. (*Begins looking through the magazines for coupons.*) Oh, this here is a fifty cents off on Miracle Whip. That's good stuff□ — that Miracle Whip. I couldn't buy it when Vern was alive. He complained that it tasted like sugar and mayonnaise.

IRIS: Well ain't that what it is?

NELLIE: I guess. (*Excitedly.*) Lookie here, I ain't seen one of these in ages!

IRIS: What?

NELLIE: A seventy-five cents off on frozen Pizza!

IRIS: It ain't microwavable.

NELLIE: How do you know?

IRIS: It's too big to fit through the door.

NELLIE: Oh. *(She crumples the coupon and tosses it on the table.)* How's the apartment hunting coming along?

IRIS: I found out exactly what four-hundred a month on social security can get. I'm goin' to see about some senior housin' next week. And by the way, don't mention my failed attempts to find an apartment to my kids—I don't want anybody's pity.

NELLIE: I may be in the same boat as you soon. My daughter brought up selling the land to the mining company again.

IRIS: She can't do that.

NELLIE: I'm serious. Why do you think I'm agreeing to your departure? Marg is gonna sell this land and put me in a home for decrepits.

IRIS: A home for who?

NELLIE: Decrepits! Old folks who pee in the bed and sing songs to their dead mothers.

IRIS: Your exaggeratin'—Marg is just talkin'.

NELLIE: Iris, when I was near death in the hospital, after my stroke, I gave Margie power of attorney over all my possessions if I should become sick again.

IRIS: Now that was plumb stupid.

NELLIE: Well, she was acting so nice to me and all. Now, every time I sneeze Marg writes it down in her little book.

IRIS: It won't happen.

NELLIE: Marg always gets what she wants, Iris. Always.

IRIS: Not this time. I better skedaddle so I can make it to town before the sun gets too hot. (*She gets purse off table.*) See ya before the cactus blooms.

NELLIE: I'll water the garden. If there's any okra, I'll fry it up for our lunch.

IRIS: Leave the watterin' to me. You got to be careful out in this heat. The air is already as hot as the inside of a horse's butt. (*Exits out side door.*)

NELLIE: (*looks at wrist watch*). Oops! Ten O'clock. Time for a drinky pooh. Ten O'clock, time for drinky pooh. (*Takes newspaper and exits into house.*)

BLACKOUT

SCENE II

(The following morning. Iris enters with salad bowl which she dumps into rabbit cage. She moves the fan from the table into the far corner and then exits into house. A few moments later, Nellie enters with water which she gives to rabbits. She notices the fan is missing, looks around for it, and puts it back where it was. After turning the fan on, she exits into house. Iris reenters with her normal breakfast fare and sits in her usual spot. Nellie follows shortly thereafter with newspaper.)

IRIS: I 'spose you watered Merle and Patsy?

NELLIE: Bone dry! (*Pause.*) I think that water bottle has a slow leak

IRIS: Reckon we should of...

NELLIE: Gotten a water bottle when we were in town. Well you were in town yesterday, why didn't you get one.

IRIS: Slipped my mind.

NELLIE: (*mocking*). Slipped my mind. All you do around here is dig in the dirt. Always out there tinkering in that garden. I could use a little help *inside* the house, Iris!

IRIS: It's not my fault you're so slovenly.

NELLIE: I am not slovenly! At least I flush the commode after relieving myself.

IRIS: You know all too well why I don't flush the damned commode!

NELLIE: Just flush the damned commode, Iris! Just flush the damned commode.

IRIS: Oh, I'll flush the damned commode alright! Right after I stick your damned head in it!

NELLIE: I can't wait until you're outta here! (*An awkward moment of silence.*) You're so good at digging why don't you dig a hole to piss in!

IRIS: (*Iris finds this last statement quite humorous*). How old were you when your folks got a bathroom?

NELLIE: We never had indoor plumbing when I was growing up. But every time we went to town, I'd ask Momma if we could visit Mrs. Olsen. I got so excited walking up those big steps thinking about the swirlin' water in Mrs. Olsen's porcelain bowl—I would just about pee in my panties thinking about it. I would wait until right before we left and I'd say: "Momma, I gotta go!" And Momma would say: "Do you mind, Mrs. Olsen?" And Mrs. Olsen would lead me to the bathroom. She walked really slow. When I shut the bathroom door, I became the queen of the castle. I'd give my speech to all the

plebeians, that means people of a lower class—
the ones who had to use outhouses, and then I'd
slowly pull down my panties and sit on the
throne.

IRIS: (*with the most possible sarcasm*). I wasn't
aware it could be a religious experience. And I
know what the word plebian means.

NELLIE: Did you find an apartment yesterday?

IRIS: Don't worry, you'll be the first to know when I
do.

NELLIE: Why don't you ask to move back in with one of
your boys?

IRIS: Oh, they've paid their dues. 'Sides, Chester just
remarried. She's a hussy of a woman! I don't
need to tell you what two women vying for the
head of household is like.

NELLIE: Well, why don't you just let her take charge?
(*Holding up a miniature teapot.*) Can you tell
what this is?

IRIS: It's a teapot. If it were that easy for two grown
women to get along in the same house, do you
think I would be in such a rush to leave here?
Hell, I'm too old to change my ways, and I
refuse to live under martial law to keep my
son's wife happy. Besides Bethany's gonna ask
me to come live with her.

NELLIE: Will you accept?

IRIS: I may have no other choice...the option would

be nice. (*Pause.*) I shot that little cottontail
yesterday.

NELLIE: In the garden again, eh?

IRIS: Took down a whole row of snap beans.

NELLIE: (*looks at the remaining banana*). You gonna...

IRIS: (*pushing the banana toward Nellie*). There's
still a few bananas on top of the fridge.

NELLIE: This'll do just fine, thank you. You know, it's
cheaper if you buy milk by the gallon.

IRIS: Yes, I know. But there ain't no room in your
refrigerator. I noticed you had thirty cans of
Vern's skoal in the side door. We could get rid
of that stuff and I'd have room for my milk.

NELLIE: No use in throwing away good tobacco.

IRIS: Vern's been dead for over a year, that tobacco is
useless.

NELLIE: I'm gonna make potpourri out of it.

IRIS: Do what?

NELLIE: It's wintergreen flavor—has a strong outdoorsy
scent.

IRIS: I said I'd find a place to live by months end, you
don't have to resort to puttin' potpourri skoal
around! (*Pause.*) I ain't heard the Cactus Wren
this mornin'.

NELLIE: Maybe she went off looking for a new man.

IRIS: No, she's got a nest out there by the turn.

NELLIE: Another good rain and that turn will be a big
wash. Vern used to keep it up so nice. All his

work has been almost completely erased by the
wind and rain.

IRIS: Did that boy down the road say he'd help you
          out around the place after I leave?

NELLIE: No, but I put up a notice at the post office.
          (*Opens her newspaper.*) How much of that
          frozen yogurt company did you buy?

IRIS: 'Bout five-thousand dollars' worth.

NELLIE: You're now up by one-thousand on that one!
          Hot dang, Iris, you sure know how to pick 'em.
          (*Getting up.*) I'd better see about finding
          something to put together for lunch.

IRIS: Let's have that frozen yogurt for dessert.

NELLIE: Is that what that stuff is? No wonder why your
          stock's doing so well! (*Exits into the house.*)

IRIS: I'll go see to the garden. (*Exits out side door.*)

NELLIE: (*offstage*). Don't leave the milk out, Iris!
          (*Enters, gets milk.*) For pity's sake. (*Smells
          milk.*) Smells like toe jam down in there!
          (*Exits.*)

BLACKOUT

SCENE III

(Lights up. The following afternoon. Bethany,
Iris's daughter sits at the table sipping a glass of
tea. The fan blows the midday heat. Iris shouts
from the kitchen.)

IRIS: This here is a new recipe I've been meanin' to
try out. Bethany, where are you? I could use a
little help here! (*Bethany jumps up to open the
door as Iris enters carrying a casserole.*) You
put wieners on the bottom, then baked beans,
some sauerkraut, and top if off with cheddar
cheese and sour cream.

BETH: You'll have to let me get a copy of that one,
Mom.

IRIS: My own sauerkraut too. I've been agin' it out
here on the porch for a few months. (*She scoops
out a big helping for Bethany.*) You just throw
cabbage in a pot, add some salt and water, put a
cheese cloth on top, and a few months later you
scrape the mold off. Voilà—sauerkraut! It's real
easy. (*Scoops out another spoonful.*)

BETH: Actually, Mom, I'm not really hungry. Is Nellie
going to eat?

IRIS: She's havin' her nap. There'll be plenty left for

her, don't you worry none. Well, back your ears and dive in!

BETH: That long drive always seems to take the hunger right out of me. Maybe I'll just have some of your fresh vegetables.

IRIS: Suit yourself. (*Takes Bethany's plate for herself.*) I guess it'll keep till dinner. Hell, it's been sittin' out here on the porch for months, it ought to last for a couple more hours.

BETH: Well I thought I would take you out to dinner tonight, Mom.

IRIS: That'll be nifty. We can have those leftovers for breakfast.

BETH: Sauerkraut for breakfast? Mom, Really?

IRIS: Honey, when you was raised as dirt poor as I was, you learn to eat whatever's lookin' ya in the face.

BETH: I know. I know. But you certainly couldn't have been any poorer than we were.

IRIS: You don't know what poor is, child. I lived in a chicken coop the first year of my life. I had one dress for six days of the week and one for Sunday.

BETH: But your parents managed to keep you, didn't they?

IRIS: (*this hits hard but she ignores it and continues*). Once my daddy caught me wearin' my Sunday dress to school...he slapped me so hard my mama knocked him unconscious with a rollin' pin. She was ahead of her time. (*Changing subjects.*) Maybe Nellie would like to come to dinner with us.

BETH: (*walking to the rabbit cage*). Just you and me, okay? I thought we would talk about...us.

IRIS: If you're worried about Nellie listenin' in, she already knows everything. It ain't no secret she wants me out of here. And I don't blame her. She's gone above and beyond the call of duty for a sister-in-law.

BETH: (*pulling rabbit out of hutch*). Merle's gotten so big! Is this one Merle?

IRIS: (*not turning around to look, still eating*). The solid white one is Merle. I've been feedin' him all the scraps from the garden.

BETH: Maybe you should put him on a diet.

IRIS: No, 'cause if he doesn't consummate with Patsy, I'm gonna make some of my famous rabbit stew. I think he might be a homosexual bunny.

BETH: (*appalled*). You can't cook a pet, Mom. You never did care about animals! (*Puts rabbit back in hutch.*) Remember the time you made me pluck Edgar? I was so angry at you for that.

IRIS: I waited two years for you to outgrow your attachment to that bird. If I had waited any longer, Edgar would have gotten too tough to eat.

BETH: Mother! I loved that turkey. Everyone loved Edgar. He was the only turkey I ever heard of that could do back flips. And knowing how much he meant to me, you still made me pluck his feathers.

IRIS: Your father was gone! We were practically starvin' for Pete's sake. You don't have to keep tellin' me what a rotten mother I was! I might not have been a saint, but I did the best I could as a widowed mother of three small children.

BETH: You mean a widowed mother of two small male children!

IRIS: You were still my daughter.

BETH: It never felt that way to me.

IRIS: I know it was hard. Life is hard. A kid might as well learn that lesson early.

BETH: With you for a mother, I learned that lesson many times. And guess what, Mom, life has never been that hard since.

IRIS: What has gotten into you? I didn't raise my kids to be so disrespectful!

BETH: My therapist thinks that I should...

IRIS: Therapist?

BETH: Yes. I've been seeing a therapist for about a year.

IRIS: So, your therapist is blamin' me for your life mistakes?

BETH: Mom, would you just listen?

IRIS: I don't want to discuss this anymore. (*Exits into trailer with dishes*.)

BETH: (*after an awkward pause*). Looks like you've lost a little weight.

IRIS: (*from kitchen*). I'm down to a size four.

BETH: Size four? You'll have to let me know where you get your dresses.

IRIS: (*reenters*). 'Course, I've always had a pretty good figure.

BETH: Isn't that what caught dad's eye?

IRIS: (*she chuckles*). That's what snagged him alright. The first time I met your father, I got my dress caught on a barbed wire fence and there I stood, almost stark naked! Silly man, he thought it was an accident. (*They both laugh*.) I had the hottest legs in Hot Springs.

BETH: Clever as a fox.

IRIS: A woman's got to be clever to survive in this world.

BETH: I never quite mastered your techniques.

IRIS: You've managed well.

BETH: No, I haven't. It's all an act. But I didn't come here to go on pretending the way we always have. I'm done. To be honest, I came here to talk about something I haven't been brave enough to bring up before. So, I'm just going to come straight out with it. I want to know why you sent me to the Baptist Children's Home.

Why me and not the boys?

IRIS: I don't want to talk about that, Beth. Not now.

BETH: I know how you feel. I've spent my whole life avoiding this discussion. Avoiding you. Fighting off the memories of my own mom sending me to live with someone else. But not anymore. We have got to talk about this...before...

IRIS: Before what? When will you kids learn that words won't change anything?

BETH: I would like a relationship with you. I long for what I never had as a child—to whatever degree it might happen now. If it's even possible. You owe me that.

IRIS: I brought you back home as soon as I could. You had plenty of time to be my daughter.

BETH: I can't go on acting like nothing happened. (*Pauses as she considers her thoughts.*) When you came to pick me up at the home that last time...I tried so hard not to look you in the face. I never wanted to look you in the face again. But when you reached for my hand, my eyes went instinctively to yours. I couldn't help it. Brown...It was the first time I remember seeing that you had brown eyes. I felt so totally at peace at that moment... warm...protected. And then you turned away. You couldn't even look at me. (*Waits for response but gets none.*) I need to be able to let this go. I want to forgive you, but I can't...unless you help me.

IRIS: Is this why you came here?

BETH: Yes, partly.

IRIS: (*with much contempt*). Then you can turn
          around and leave.

NELLIE:(*enters from house*). Well, surprise, surprise!
          How are you doing Beth?

BETH: Hi, Aunt Nellie. I'm fine, thanks.

IRIS: (*rising from her chair*). If you two will excuse
          me, I'm goin' to see if I turned the water off in
          the garden. (*Exits out side door.*)

NELLIE:I don't know what she's gonna do without a
          garden! She spends hours out there digging and
          such. When it comes to gardening, your mom is
          like a kid in a candy store.

BETH: Mom always loved her garden.

NELLIE: (*sensing something is wrong*). Beth, you know
          I never asked your mom to leave. She's got it in
          her head that it's time for her to move on.

BETH: I know, Aunt Nellie. You don't need to explain.
          Mom is a stubborn lady.

NELLIE:You gonna stay a spell? You know you're more
          than welcome.

BETH: (*looking towards the front yard*). I have to
          leave Sunday afternoon.

NELLIE:(*moves next to Bethany, stands by her side*).
          That's too bad. Iris loves your visits so. But I
          reckon a weekend is better than nothing. Did

you taste her sauerkraut?

(*They both laugh. Nellie wraps an arm around Bethany and squeezes.*) It's really good to see you again.

BETH: Thank you, Nellie. I don't know what I would do without you.

NELLIE: If you ever need a shoulder, I'm always here.

BETH: (*still gazing outside*). The prickly pears are gone. The whole batch—cleared away.

NELLIE: I always hated those things being so close to my carport, but Vern wouldn't get rid of them. He couldn't bring himself to kill any cactus on the whole five acres.

BETH: Tell me! Remember the first time us kids met Uncle Vern? We were throwing rocks at those very prickly pears and he came out with his shotgun and told us to get the hell off his property if we couldn't respect what was here before us. Vern always scared the bejesus out of me.

NELLIE: Scared the bejesus outta me too. (*Slight pause.*) I had them transplanted. I guess I'm a lot like Vern. I love this land and everything on it with all my soul. I would just as soon die as give up this place.

BETH: Vern is still here, isn't he?

NELLIE: Can you feel him?

BETH: I can.

NELLIE: In the plants, the trees, the soil. He put his whole being into this place. And look at it...the well is going dry again. The septic tank is actin' up. And the wolves keep digging holes everywhere.

BETH: Maybe he's trying to tell you something.

NELLIE: Who?

BETH: Uncle Vern. Maybe he thinks it's time for you to move on. This place is too much for you to keep up by yourself.

NELLIE: I'm going to start interviewing for someone to help out around here in exchange for a little food and money.

BETH: Good idea. I know we would all feel better if someone were here to watch over you. (*Margie, Nellie's daughter, enters through the side door. She has very short bleach blond hair that has been permed one too many times. A camel cigarette hangs from her mouth. Her skin is dry and weathered from the Arizona sun. She sets a small overstuffed suitcase on the floor and tosses a small brown paper bag on the table.*)

MARG: (*to Bethany*). Look who the cat drug in! Bethany! How's my favorite cousin? (*Looks her up and down.*) I heard you had put on a little weight, but I thought I'd wait to see for myself before dispersing any rumors. Don't worry though, you probably won't ever get a big as your mom. Too much fried food I tell her. You don't fry your food, do you? Well, listen to me go on and on. How are you? And where is that good lookin' eyetalian feller of yours? (*Not waiting for her to answer.*) Can he still put away the wine? Mom, remember Dominick at Dad's funeral? What a lively fella' he was. Course I don't know if it was such a good idea to be drinking so much at a funeral...but you know alcoholics and eyetalians. Oh, I'm not alleging Dominick is an alcoholic. Course it's very in now—to be addicted to drink. It's the clean poison they say. (*She opens her arms wide.*) Well, aren't you even going to give me a hug?

BETH: (*forces a smile and hugs Margie*). What a pleasant surprise.

MARG: Mom told me you were heading down so I thought I would skedaddle on over too. Aren't you excited? (*Margie fondles Bethany's ear.*) I simply adore these earrings.

BETH: (*pulling away*). Thanks. I love what you've done to your hair.

NELLIE: I told her to stop with those home perms.

MARG: (*ignoring her mother.*) The sun lightens it you know.

NELLIE: What are you talking about? The sun didn't do that.

MARG: (*shoots her mom a look*). How do you know what the sun does? (*Quickly changes subjects.*) You got the swamp cooler on in the trailer? (*To Bethany.*) Let's go inside where it's nice and cool to catch up, Beth. It's been so long. (*She grabs Bethany's hand and pulls her towards the door. She stops midway and looks at her mom.*) Mom, I brought you some bath gels. Lilac—isn't that your favorite? Help yourself. They're in the bag on the table. (*Looks back to Bethany.*) I like to bring her little surprises. (*Bethany and Margie exit into the trailer. Nellie plops down in the nearest chair and sighs. Iris enters through the side door.*)

IRIS & NELLIE: (*in unison*). Marg!

IRIS: Did she bring the dog?

NELLIE: Now don't start getting in a tizzy, Iris!

IRIS: That dog always has the perpetual runs! I think Marg scares the shit right out of him.

NELLIE: She didn't bring the dog you foul mouthed ol' coot! What's going on with you and Beth?

IRIS: She doesn't want me to live with her.

NELLIE: Did she say that?

IRIS: She didn't have to. Said she's seein' a psychiatrist.

NELLIE: Good for her. She's a good kid—deserves to be happy.

IRIS: Why do you always make me feel like a lousy

mother?

NELLIE: I do no such thing. You did the best you could under the circumstances. (*Margie opens door, unnoticed by the others. She hesitates in order to eavesdrop.*)

IRIS: No, I didn't. I should have found a way to keep all of them together. I just couldn't afford all three of them. And I never was any good with girls. I should have stopped after the boys.

NELLIE: Stop? What do you mean stop? You had a choice? Had my brother not died so young you would have probably ended up with a brood as big as mine. (*Iris notices Margie who acts as though she just opened the door. She enters with a large glass in her hand.*)

MARG: Hello, Iris. Mom, who has been drinking all the vodka? Iris, have you been slurping down the good stuff?

NELLIE: I thought you went inside to visit with Bethany.

MARG: It's too damn hot in there. Swamp cooler must be broke. Bethany's taking a bath anyway. A bath at this hour. I told her not to run the well dry. With Iris hosing down the garden every day, you two may have to start sucking the juice out of those tomatoes. You're looking very lovely today, Iris.

IRIS: (*walks past Margie towards front door*). Thank you, Marg. I'll see if Bethany needs any towels. (*She exits.*)

NELLIE: (*looks into Margie's glass and fans her nose*).
What do you mean, where'd the vodka go?

MARG: I had to make up for the lack of orange juice.

NELLIE: There wasn't any orange juice.

MARG: That's what I mean.

NELLIE: I don't see how you can drink that stuff straight.

MARG: I came by it honestly. (*Sits next to her mom.*)
How have you been feeling?

NELLIE: Fit as a fiddle.

MARG: Really? That's good. Have you thought about
my proposition?

NELLIE: (*harshly, but in a quite tone as not to be
overheard*). I'm not selling the land, Margie.
That's all there is to it.

MARG: You don't have to snap at me! I think us kids
have some say in this. After all, it was our
father's land too.

NELLIE: This land was never your father's. It was your
father's and mine.

MARG: Why should you sit way out here when you
could be in town close to all the doctors and
stuff?

NELLIE: This is my home, Margie. Don't you understand
that?

MARG: Of course I do. But just imagine if you were in a
retirement center. You would have lots of
friends and you could take ceramics. I would

just love to have a ceramic ashtray, Mom. Will you make me an ashtray?

NELLIE: What in the hell are you talking about?

MARG: I think you're being awful selfish. The mining company offered us a lot of money for this place. An offer like that won't last long.

NELLIE: So, what do you think, Margie? That all the proceeds will go to you?

MARG: Of course not. It would all go to the nursing home...most likely.

NELLIE: Nursing home? What happened to retirement center? I'm not selling the land and that's final!

MARG: The doctor's say you shouldn't be living out here by yourself.

NELLIE: Iris is here.

MARG: The blind leading the blind. Besides, she's leaving. Iris is smart enough to know this place is too much to handle.

NELLIE: Don't you worry. I'm going to hire someone to help out around here.

MARG: Don't fight this, Mom. It's inevitable. I'm just thinking of your best interest.

NELLIE: All you're thinking about is the money!
(*Obviously shaken and emotional, Nellie stands, gets her cane, and walks outside.*)

MARG: (*yelling towards the door*). I don't know where you get those ideas, Maw. Don't you realize I'm doing this because I love you? No one else has the guts to tell you the truth.

NELLIE: (*offstage*). I won't leave my home, Margie.

MARG: (*lights a cigarette. Walks over to trailer door and sticks her head in.*) Where is the ladder, Iris? I'm going to climb up on the roof and fix that damn swamp cooler. (*She slams the door, not waiting for a response.*) Never mind, I'll find it myself. (*Sits her drink down and exits outside.*)

IRIS: (*enters with bowl of food for rabbits. Opens side door on way to rabbit cage, yells to Margie*). The ladder is in the shed closest to the water hose. (*Walks over to rabbit cage and dumps food in. She shakes water bottle.*) Empty again! (*She takes Margie's glass of vodka and fills the water bottle. She places the water bottle back in the cage.*)

LIGHTS FADE

SCENE IV

(The sun is setting. The patio table is dressed
for supper with a colorful cloth. A string of
lights in the shape of red chili peppers hangs
from above. The fan blows. Margie is sitting
with her leg propped on a table, it is bandaged.
Bethany sits next to Nellie. Iris sits in the
center.)

IRIS: (*passing bowl to Margie*). I really am sorry I
           forgot to tell you about that top step.

NELLIE: You should get to a doctor about that.

MARG: (*glaring at Iris*). I'm leaving first thing in the
           morning.

IRIS: (*reacting to Margie's glare*). What did I do?

NELLIE: Here, Margie, have some more wine. It'll reduce
           the swelling.

MARG: Don't mind if I do. (*Pours herself a glass.*)

BETH: This is great soup, Aunt Nellie. What is it?

NELLIE: Your mom made it.

BETH: (*surprised*). Really? It's great, Mom. The meat
           is really tender.

MARG: And tasty.

IRIS: Thank you.

MARG: Haven't you found a place to live yet, Iris?

NELLIE: Margie!

MARG: Well? Let's face it, you don't have enough money to feed Iris forever.

IRIS: I'm exploring my options.

MARG: What options?

BETH: No need to wait, Mom. I'll help you look for a place while I'm here. We can go out tomorrow.

IRIS: (*hurt but trying to cover*). I think I'm going to retire. I don't think the soup agreed with me.

NELLIE: I'll clean up the dishes.

IRIS: (*slowly exiting*). See you in the mornin'.

BETH: Are you okay?

IRIS: Just need to rest, that's all. (*She exits.*)

MARG: Of course, I don't blame you, Beth. Your mom would be way too hard to live with. She might drive that eyetalian feller of yours right out of the house.

NELLIE: (*to Bethany*). Iris thought you were going to ask her to come live with you.

MARG: Everyone knows how wrong she did you. It's amazing you grew up worth anything at all. Kids with your background usually end up on drugs or something. You did real good for yourself, Beth. Mom and I are real proud of you.

BETH: That's nice of you to say, Margie. I hate to admit it, but you're right. (*Rising from table.*) I'm not sure Mom and I could live together. She makes me so nervous.

MARG: Oh, please! Beth, you don't owe your mom

anything. Don't worry yourself about it. Are we supposed to be responsible for our parents? I don't think so. Iris should have planned ahead. Now she's caught in old age without any money. What? Is that your fault? I don't think so.

NELLIE: Then why don't you stop taking such "good care" of me!

BETH: Aunt Nellie? Why is the door to the rabbit hutch open? (*Peers inside the cage.*) Merle is missing.

NELLIE: (*standing behind Bethany*). They were awful rambunctious this afternoon. Maybe they jolted the door open. Merle will come back when he's hungry.

MARG: (*smirking, picking her teeth with a toothpick*). Or when we have leftovers.

BETH: What do you mean, Margie?

MARG: Iris told me she was making rabbit stew.

NELLIE: Iris would never cook Merle.

BETH: She will never change! How could she do that?

MARG: I don't know, I thought Merle was mighty tasty...

NELLIE: (*somewhat confused, looks around the porch for traces of the rabbit*). Merle...Come here baby. Where are you? Merle? (*Bethany helps Nellie look for the rabbit. She checks the door, testing how easily a rabbit could push it open.*)

MARG: You have cats at your place, don't ya, Bethany?

BETH: Two.

MARG: Yeah, I'd be careful about moving Iris into my house if I was you.

BETH: Shut up Margie. (*She steps outside.*) Maybe he was able to get the door open.

NELLIE: Yeah, that's it. He must've hopped outside when we were hoisting Marg's fat butt in after her fall.

MARG: That's not very nice, Mom!

NELLIE: Oh, I'm just teasing you. Lighten up. Well, we may as well finish eating. He'll come back. You'll see. (*All three are seated but reserved about eating. Margie lifts up her spoon and then reconsiders. Bethany pushes her bowl away. Nellie attempts to eat in order to prove it is not Merle, but fails.*) Dessert anyone? I made a delicious carrot cake.

MARG: (*laughing hysterically*). Carrot cake, how ironic. (*Bethany shakes her head and Nellie looks as though she is about to cry. Margie stops laughing.*) I'm not really hungry.

BETH: Me either.

NELLIE: Carrots were Merle's favorite.

BETH: I'm terribly sorry, Aunt Nellie.

NELLIE: Oh, it was just a dumb ol' rabbit! One less responsibility.

MARG: Which reminds me, I want to tell you about some of the nursing homes I contacted.

NELLIE: Don't be too hasty. I don't think you hurt your leg that badly. You should still be able to take care of yourself. (*Bethany conceals a laugh.*)

MARG: (*ignores Nellie's joke*). There's one in
Oklahoma...that's real affordable. Nursing
homes are so damned expensive out here.

NELLIE: Oklahoma!

MARG: That's where you were born. I figured it be like
going home.

NELLIE: I haven't been back to Oklahoma since I was
four years old.

MARG: What would happen if you had another stroke?
It's an hour's drive to the nearest hospital. I
won't have that guilt on my conscience. (*Short
Pause.*) I recall when the plumbing went out a
couple of summers ago and you ventured
outside in the dark to take a dump. Right smack
dab on top of a barrel cactus!

NELLIE: It could happen to anyone.

MARG: Dad said your butt looked like an antique dart
board.

NELLIE: (*walking away*). I've managed all this time
without any help from you.

MARG: And now I'm here to help.

NELLIE: Like a vulture lookin' for highway pizza!

MARG: Stop it, Mom! Do you think this is easy for me?
What? Do you think I like doing this? I don't,
okay? Alright? I hate this. I hate dealing with
this, but no one else has the guts to do what
they know is necessary. Let's face it, you and I

have never gotten along anyway. So, what have I got to lose? A relationship with my mother? I think not. (*After a short pause, Margie regains her composure.*) If it will make you feel any better, I'll look for a nursing home closer to here.

NELLIE: My first interview for a caretaker is next week.

MARG: You're not listening, Mother.

NELLIE: Oh, I hear you just fine.

MARG: It's over. You can't stay here any longer. That's all there is to it.

NELLIE: (*moving towards side door, gazing out*). Your dad and I wore that path up to the garden. He loved working with the dirt on this land. It's all he had that he could call his own. Kids grow up and leave. Homes and cars deteriorate. But the land...it remains through the seasons. (*Pauses.*) Your dad and I placed every stone along the road. With our bare hands. It took about ten years to line the entire drive, but there was no hurry. There was plenty of time. (*Walks over to other side of porch for another view of yard.*) I've still got to finish putting the rocks around the new shed. Rains come hard once about every ten years. Need to place the rocks so the water will wash away from the foundation. Of course, the netting needs to be redone on the ...that old totem pole...that funny looking

contraption...the pots and pans on the well
cover. People always take pictures when they
come visit. Haven't seen Glen in a while. (*Stops
and looks at Nellie.*) Have you seen Glen? Do
you remember when he got caught up in the
barbed wire with that wild horse? What was
that horse's name? (*She stops and stares into
space.*)

MARG: Maw?

NELLIE: Outlaw. Called him Outlaw.

MARG: Don't make this hard on me, Mom.

NELLIE: I would like for you to leave now, Margie.
You're not welcome on this land. Outlaw says
you're not welcome here anymore.

MARG: Outlaw? What?

NELLIE: Leave! Now! Take your bags and leave. You're
not welcome here anymore.

MARG: You're going to kick your own daughter out of
your house?

NELLIE: Yes, out of *my* house.

MARG: Plumb crazy! That's what you are. You wait till I
tell Carol about this. She told me you were losin'
it, but I thought you might have a little time left.
(*Hurt, trying not to cry.*) This is not a dead
issue. This was Dad's house too, and he would
be ashamed of how you are behaving. (*Marg
storms inside the house. Nellie struggles to
remain strong. She quickly grabs a napkin off

the table to dry her eyes. Marg returns with bag in hand.*) Have a good life! (*She exits and then yells from offstage.*) Oww! Shit! Shit! Shit! (*She reenters with her arm sticking out, it is covered in cactus thorns.*) Since when was there a prickly pear patch next to my parking spot!

NELLIE: Wait here and I'll go get the pliers. (*She exits inside.*)

MARG: Hurry! And bring some peroxide. (*Margie attempts to pull out a few quills on her own. She whimpers like a small child.*)

NELLIE: (*quickly reenters and immediately attends to Margie*). It's kind of late to be driving. You may as well stay the night. (*Margie says nothing as Nellie removes the remaining thorns.*)

MARG: (*walks to side door and after opening it, turns back towards her mother*). Tell Bethany I'll give her a call. I think I've made my position quite clear. (*She exits. Nellie walks over to rabbit hutch and picks up Patsy.*)

LIGHTS FADE

SCENE V

(One month later. A rainy day in September. Lights come up on porch. Sounds of rain and occasional thunder can be heard. The door to the trailer opens. Nellie enters with a salad bowl and a bottle of water which she gives to the rabbit.)

NELLIE: Getting pretty lonely in there is it? Don't you worry, Patsy, you'll start cottonin' to the solitude. It's not like you and Merle were having relations anyway. Oh, you don't need to tell me about that. Vern and I stopped having relations years ago. Perhaps Merle had problems in that area. I never did see that rabbit excited—if you know what I mean. I'm beginning to think that Iris cut his doodle bug off so he would get nice and fat. Of course, Vern never got fat. And he did still have his doodle bug. He just lost interest. Not that Merle lost interest in you. Men are strange creatures, Patsy. As young men they rise to every occasion. When they get older, they can't even remember what the occasion was.

(*A young man enters with a chair. He is in good shape but average in stature. He wears a red checkered shirt and brown pants. His hair is neatly combed, matching his well-kept appearance. He has a Mexican accent, but speaks English well.*)

JIMMY: (*holding chair*). Finished. Just like new.

NELLIE: (*standing on the front steps of the front door*). Wonderful. It sure looks pretty.

JIMMY: I better get home now. You need anything else?

NELLIE: No. Do you want some dinner before you leave?

JIMMY: Thank you, no. Graciela always has lunch ready for me.

NELLIE: How about some pie?

JIMMY: (*hesitant but wanting to appease her*). Okay.

NELLIE: (*exits into trailer. She speaks through kitchen window*). The garden looks well-tended to. I went to take a look yesterday.

JIMMY: Gracias. You should be careful going outside when not feeling well. And you should stop letting that rabbit loose in the garden.

NELLIE: What do you mean?

JIMMY: I know you've been letting that fat rabbit eat the tomato plants.

NELLIE: (*reenters, hands small plate of pie to Jimmy*). It must be the wild rabbits.

JIMMY: (*points to cage*). It's that rabbit. He even smells

like tomatoes.

NELLIE: Well aren't you quite the detective. God loves rabbits too.

JIMMY: (*smiling*). Yes, he does. (*Sits down at the table and pokes a fork into his pie.*)

NELLIE: Well, aren't you going to eat your prickly pear pie? Iris made it while she was visiting yesterday.

JIMMY: (*nibbles, obviously uncertain about the pie*). Iris? Can I get this to go?

NELLIE: Sure. I'll send the whole thing home with you. Maybe your Grace would like to try some.

JIMMY: That won't be necessary. Graciela doesn't like pie.

NELLIE: Well, she can't live off tamales and burritos alone. You let her try it.

JIMMY: Okay. Thank you.

NELLIE: (*sits down next to Jimmy, begins clipping coupons*). You eat picante sauce, don't you?

JIMMY: Sure, sometimes.

NELLIE: Here's a fifty cents off coupon. (*Hands it to him.*)

JIMMY: Fifty cents? Wow. Thank you.

NELLIE: It's never about how much you make, Jimmy. It's about how you take care of what you have. Let Grace know that the grocery store has double coupon days on Wednesday.

JIMMY: I'll let her know.

NELLIE: I think you are a special man for marrying her.
You're so young and she already came with a
two-year-old. Taking on someone else's kid
can't be easy.

JIMMY: I prayed about it.

NELLIE: You did?

JIMMY: Put it in the hands of the Lord. It was His choice
that we marry. You should talk to God. He will
answer your questions. You are close to meeting
him, no?

NELLIE: How old do you think I am?

JIMMY: Eighty-two?

NELLIE: I reckon God appreciates your honesty, but it
wouldn't be a mortal sin to shave off a few
years, would it? (*Short pause.*) Jimmy, why
does someone like you help an old lady like me?

JIMMY: I need the money.

NELLIE: It barely pays for the gas to come all the way out
here.

JIMMY: If I help you, you get to stay here, yes? (*Nellie
nods in agreement.*) You can't take care of this
place by yourself.

NELLIE: That still doesn't answer my question.

JIMMY: You no like the answer.

NELLIE: How you know I no like the answer?

JIMMY: I'm here because you need help. That's all.

NELLIE: (*shaking her head*). Everyone has their reasons.

JIMMY: You need to believe in people again, Mrs. Brye.

Maybe that is why I am here. When would you like me to come back?

NELLIE: Mañana?

JIMMY: Si, mañana. (*Jimmy rises to leave.*)

NELLIE: Wait. (*She pulls an envelope from her pocket.*) Here's your check.

JIMMY: (*takes check and after looking at it, shakes his head*). No, Mrs. Brye, this is too much. (*He holds out check, but she pushes his hand away.*)

NELLIE: You stop in Green Valley and get Grace a hanging basket—one with flowers.

JIMMY: (*he nods gratefully, places check in his pocket*). Thank you.

NELLIE: And take that chair with you.

JIMMY: Your chair?

NELLIE: What do I need with another chair? Take it. You can't use it?

JIMMY: No, we can use it. Thank you, Mrs. Brye. You are a good lady. You should come to church with me and the family on Sunday. (*He opens side door, with chair and pie in hand.*) I'll pick you up. God bless you. (*He exits.*)

NELLIE: (*she watches Jimmy walk to his truck. She waves one last time. She walks over to rabbit hutch and speaks to Patsy*). You stop it with those tomatoes! That Jimmy is a good boy. But I sure wish he would stop it with all that religion stuff. Me and the Lord—we got it right with each other. He's already reserved me a spot on the other side of the pearly gates. (*Walks back over to table and folds up a lawn chair. She then exits up steps into trailer only to quickly reenter with a banana. She walks back to table, sets the banana down, and puts the lawn chair back out.*) Never know who might stop by. It's a shame to waste half this banana. They just won't keep. (*Looks towards Patsy.*) No, you can't have it. (*Walks downstage and looks out into yard.*) What a glorious day! I adore monsoon season. The smell of the rain on the desert sand. The sound of monster rain drops cloppin' on the hard, thirsty ground. When it clears up, I'll take you to the garden. Wouldn't that give Iris palpitations. Serves her right. It just upsets me so—that she wouldn't admit to cookin' Merle. Born during the depression. Old rabbits die hard—habits, old *habits* die hard. Can't say as I'm gonna hold it against her, especially since I can't really say for certain she did it. (*She turns to walk inside.*) Welp, twelve o'clock. Time for a drinky pooh...twelve o'clock...time for a drinky pooh. (*She looks back at Patsy.*) See you after my nap.

BLACKOUT

SCENE VI

(*The porch is decorated with lights and balloons. It is late afternoon, a week later. There is a large "Congratulations" sign on the front door. Nellie and Jimmy sit at table as Iris enters from the trailer with cake in hand. She places cake on table and picks up a glass to make a toast.*)

IRIS: Hear, hear, this is to my sister-in-law, Nellie Brye, who has managed to hang on to her homestead by convincing everyone she is of sound mind and body. (*They all drink.*)

NELLIE: (*stands*). And here is to Iris, who went to the doctor in my place! (*They laugh and take another sip.*)

IRIS: And here's to Jimmy who takes care of this place as if it were his own. (*They drink again, followed by claps and hoots.*)

NELLIE: (*almost to tears*). I don't know how to thank you two for being so kind to me. I couldn't have pulled it off without either of you. No one can make me leave my home. No one. Not ever! (*She hugs Jimmy.*) I'm sorry your wife couldn't make it today. (*She moves to Iris.*) We have had our disagreements in the past but I want you to know—you're my dearest and oldest friend.

IRIS: Oh, cow-pies! I'm your only friend and that's by default—everyone else has died. We are stuck with each other, Nellie.

NELLIE: True. Why don't you come back here and live with me, Iris? There's plenty of room, and I would like the company.

IRIS: I'm the only friend you have left. You want to lose me too? (*Turns to look at Jimmy.*) She's a mule of a woman to live with, Jimmy.

NELLIE: Me? Why you're just as ornery as a donkey with a bumble bee up his butt! Always moving things around. Leaving the milk out. Not flushing the commode. And cooking pet rabbits!

IRIS: How many times do I have to tell you? I did not cook Merle. (*Looks at Jimmy.*) And I didn't flush the commode because she was always complainin' about the well runnin' dry. Don't mind her, Jimmy, she's just old and senile...was born a decade before me.

NELLIE: Oh, snot! I'm barely a year older.

IRIS: Yes, but you were born in an earlier decade.

NELLIE: You ol' goat! (*They both chuckle.*)

IRIS: I'm just glad you're managin' things around here. You were right. (*She pats Jimmy on the back.*) He's a good man.

JIMMY: Thank you, Iris.

NELLIE: (*a bird chirps and Nellie looks out at yard*).
Shh. (*In a hushed tone.*) There she is. She's
come back—the Inca Dove.

IRIS: Must be a different one.

NELLIE: The babies are all grown and gone. The last one
flew away weeks ago. Sally was so depressed.

JIMMY: Sally?

IRIS: She names em'. Names every bird for a quarter
of an acre.

NELLIE: (*still looking out*). After the last little one left
the nest, she sat on the highest point of that
saguaro for three straight days. Looking in
every direction for her babies. With the hot sun
beating down on her. They didn't need her.
Their wings carried them far away. I once saw
her fight off a big crow, defending her little
ones. Must've been four times her size, but she
kept at him until he left. (*She puts her hand to
her mouth as if surprised.*) My goodness. And
now her special man is back...there he is (*She
points.*) See him? Right there next to the well
cover.

IRIS: Well, where in the hell was that dead beat when
the crow came swoopin' down to eat her
hatchlings? That's what I'd like to know.

JIMMY: He was around. The female doesn't need the
male after the eggs hatch. But he helps. Even

IRIS: gathers most of the material for the nest. They mate for life, you know. When the time is right, he comes back.

IRIS: To knock her up again, no doubt!

NELLIE: Have you ever seen two birds in love, Iris? Come here.

IRIS: (*walks towards Nellie*). He's beatin' the hell out of her.

NELLIE: He's preening her. And that there... (*She smiles.*) That's their courtship dance. Just look at how much they love one another. (*Pauses.*) Why don't you find someone to do that with, Iris?

IRIS: What are you talkin' about? At my age?

NELLIE: You're healthy and agile.

IRIS: That may well be, but none of the men my age are.

NELLIE: Jimmy's grandfather-in-law is single.

JIMMY: (*somewhat nervous*). No, bueno, vive tan lejos y tendría que acercarse...He is not Iris's type.

IRIS: Don't you worry none, Jimmy. I'm not in the market for a man.

NELLIE: (*still looking at birds*). But look at those two. (*Jimmy joins the two women as they all three gaze out at the birds. They are so distracted that no one notices Margie on the other side of the yard.*)

MARG: (*yells from offstage*). Maw? Where are you? I

don't know how you convinced those doctors that you were well enough. (*Opens screen door and is surprised to see Iris and Jimmy.*) Hello, everyone.

NELLIE: Hello, Margie. (*Nellie and Margie stare at each other without saying a word.*)

IRIS: (*breaking the silence*). Jimmy, this is Marg, Nellie's daughter. Marg, this is Jimmy, Nellie's savior.

JIMMY: (*extends his hand, they shake*). Actually, I just help out around here. It's nothing really.

IRIS: Stop being so modest. He's here every single day and works for slave wages. Sometimes he won't even accept any money at all.

MARG: Aren't you dear. (*She looks at him with disdain.*) I just happen to have a bag of clothes out in the trunk of my car. Was going to give them to the mission, but it looks like you could use them more. (*She pulls keys out of her pocket and hands them to Jimmy.*) Here, you go get them and you can work it off here at my Mom and Dad's place.

JIMMY: Thank you but I don't need... (*Iris motions for him not to argue.*) Thank you for your generosity. (*He exits out screen door, followed by Iris.*)

IRIS: While you're out here, I want to show you where the extra gardening tools are kept. (*She *exits.*)

MARG: Well, aren't you going to say anything?

NELLIE: What do you want, Margie?

MARG: I don't want anything. I came over here to apologize.

NELLIE: Yes?

MARG: I'm sorry.

NELLIE: Thank you.

MARG: I'm sorry you fought me so hard on this.

NELLIE: Oh, Marg, you should congratulate me.

MARG: For what?

NELLIE: The Bible says that we shall reap what we sow. And, well, Margie, your crop is looking mighty bare right about now. But I want to tell you— don't ever regret anything you did to me. I regretted much about how I treated my mom. I never really appreciated her enough and certainly could have spent more time with her. But don't you dare do that. Don't ever feel guilty...just try to do better.

MARG: I came over her to apologize, not because I felt what I did was wrong, but because I know I hurt you. (*Exits into trailer to make a drink. Speaks offstage, occasionally through window.*) Don't forget I am a result of your care. You're my mother. You're the only person in the world that really understands me, and still accepts me...just as I am. How can I not love you? Who

47

do you think got everyone else to let you stay here after Dad died? I knew you needed some time. (*Reenters with drink in hand.*) So, don't try to put me on a guilt trip.

NELLIE: The result of *my* care? Yes, I cared for you and I loved you as much as I loved any of your brothers and sisters.

MARG: Don't try and act like you were this loving figure of a mother. You never gave me anything, especially attention. You were too busy fending off Dad to be a real parent. A drunk father and a codependent mother. God! Sometimes I resent the hell out of my kids because I bring them over here and you are nothing but good to them. Nothing but kind. Why? What is so different now that you can afford to be so wonderful?

NELLIE: Gave you things? That's what would have made you happy?

MARG: When Beth came to live with us, the first thing you did was run out and buy her a dress. A dress with lace and beautiful cherry red trim. The most beautiful dress I had ever seen.

NELLIE: My God, Margie. The poor girl had no home, no self-esteem. She needed to know that someone cared—that no matter what had happened to her, she was still special and loved.

MARG: You never told me I was special.

NELLIE: You had a family that loved and wanted you. You had everything Bethany didn't. Yet, you wanted more?

MARG: All I wanted was for you to look at me—the way you looked at her.

NELLIE: I don't know what you mean.

MARG: (*this hits Margie hard. For the first time she realizes her mom has a very different view of their relationship*). Yes, you do. (*After a short pause.*) I'm going to do what's right here. Everyone will know how much I'm trying to take care of you. No one will ever doubt how much I loved my mother, despite the fact that she never really loved me.

NELLIE: If you really loved me, you would be doing everything in your power to let me live out my days here. You shouldn't worry because there can't really be that many days left anyway. Right, Margie? (*She waits but there is no response.*) I don't want to leave everyone here. They won't survive without me. They need me here. I beg you Margie. Please, I have never asked you for anything. Just let me stay here until I die. Vern needs me. Sometimes I hear him. Sometimes he talks to me. Sometimes I see you kids running around the house—out of the corner of my eye. I turn really quick, but of course they've already gone. They run so fast, you know. They love me. That's all I have left. Don't you understand?

MARG: This place is nothing but a bunch of memories.

NELLIE: That's all we are, Margie. Haven't you figured that out? That's all we are.

MARG: What? What are we?

NELLIE: Memories. Does that mean anything to you?

MARG: You know I've never been the emotional type. I've always had to be the practical one.

NELLIE: (*with a sense of sadness*). Yes, your tears were always slow to fall.

MARG: You're thinking of no one but yourself. But of course, that's always been the way with you. Quit acting like a child, Mother. A greedy selfish child. Think of me for a change.

NELLIE: I'm not leaving.

MARG: I don't have time for this right now. I've got to get home. (*She crosses to screen door.*) When I figure out how you fooled that doctor, I'll be back to help you pack your bags. (*She exits.*)

NELLIE: (*crosses to door and steps halfway out*). What can I say to make you change your mind? (*She steps back on the porch and closes the door. She follows Margie with her eyes as she walks to her car. She speaks softly, almost mumbling.*) I'm throwing Iris a birthday party next month. I hope you can...make... (*The sound of Margie's car can be heard driving off.*

Nellie becomes slightly disoriented as she grabs her chest and awkwardly eases into the nearest chair.)

BLACKOUT

END OF ACT I

ACT II

SCENE I

IRIS: (*speaking to Patsy as she attempts to push and pull the table towards the rabbit hutch*). This way I can just feed you scraps directly from the table. (*She sits to take a break, fans herself.*) Patsy, I want you to know I had nothin' to do with Merle's disappearance. You must miss him somethin' awful. But don't take his leavin' you personal. Heck, men are always jumpin' away from me too. How old are you, Patsy? (*After a short pause.*) Yeah, I wouldn't answer that question either. (*She laughs to herself.*) As I recall, you're gettin' on up there though. I don't reckon you've done any thinkin' on your memorial services? Do you want to be cremated or put in the ground? I don't feel completely right about lettin' anyone burn my body. What would be left for the resurrection? But then the thought of me takin' up five feet of space for so long doesn't set well either. If they were to burn me and scatter my ashes over the desert, folks could see me in the sunset. A beautiful orange spectacle. That's what causes the color of the desert sunset, you know: the ashes of dead people. That's what my mom always told me. Can you imagine tellin' a ten-year-old such a thing. For years I'd start bawlin' every time the sun went down. (*Pause.*) The desert dust makes those passionate colors dance in front of the tired sun. Now that I'm not long for this world, I'm thinkin' maybe Mom was right. We are made of dust after all. Perhaps twinklin' in front of that sleepy ball of fire that burns my desert to life would be the best of grand finales. (*The screen door opens, startling Iris. Jimmy enters.*)

JIMMY: Are you talking to God, Iris? That is good. He listens to those who know His spirit.

IRIS: Well, actually I was talkin' to…Yeah, I was talkin' to God.

JIMMY: What happened here?

IRIS: The place needed a little sprucin' up. With Nellie gone, it was the perfect opportunity.

JIMMY: I don't know. I have a feeling she'll have me working overtime to put the place back the way it was. But now that you're here again, maybe we can leave it for a while. (*He pulls up a chair next to Iris.*)

IRIS: Oh, I'm not stayin'. I'm only here until Nellie gets better.

JIMMY: You must like your new apartment.

IRIS: It's a little camper over at the mobile home park, but it suits my needs.

JIMMY: They don't allow campers at the mobile home park, Iris. I see homeless people every day. I can tell when a person doesn't have a place to rest.

IRIS: (*hesitant*). The council for the aging is findin' me a place that I can afford. The waiting list is long but they said they would see what they could do.

JIMMY: I happen to know that Nellie would like it if you came back here.

IRIS: I don't need any handouts. How was she doin' this morning?

JIMMY: She was asleep and the nurse wanted her to rest. I will go back when I finish up here. You want to come with me?

IRIS: Hospitals and me don't get along. I'll see her when she gets out. How much longer does she have to stay?

JIMMY: I don't know. No more than a few days. One of her sons was there last night, but he didn't tell me what the doctor said. I don't think they like me much.

IRIS: Of course they don't. You're a decent person who's doin' what they should be a doin'. They hate your guts. Every time they see you, they feel guilty.

JIMMY: I will pray for them. (*He gets on his knees to pray.*)

IRIS: What on earth?

JIMMY: Join me, if you wish. Whenever two or more gather in His name, He is there.

IRIS: Hon, If I kneel down like that, you'll have to *gather* me up off the floor!

JIMMY: (*stands*). We can stand.

IRIS: I've got vertigo—can't close my eyes or I may stumble.

JIMMY: You pray with me and you won't stumble. I promise you this.

IRIS: Oh, hell. All right. What are you anyway, a Baptist?

JIMMY: A Christian.

IRIS: (*standing*). Yeah, go on.

JIMMY: (*reaches out for her hand*). Give me your hand.

IRIS: Didn't know we was bein' so formal.

JIMMY: La mano porfavor. (*Iris reluctantly complies. They bow their heads. After a moment of silence, Iris looks up.*)

IRIS: Well?

JIMMY: The Lord hears my thoughts.

IRIS: Then what the hell did you need me for?

JIMMY: Would you like to say a prayer?

IRIS: Bow your head. Let me show you how it's done. (*They both bow.*) Dear Lord above, Creator of heaven and earth, Jimmy and I come before you to ask that you watch over our dear Nellie Brye. Forgive us our debts, Father, and bless our loved ones. Your will be done. In your Son's name we pray, Amen.

JIMMY: Alleluia! Praise God! Bless Nellie, Father, and watch over her friend, Iris. Praise God. Hallelujah! Hallelujah. Praise the Lord. Praise God. (*Iris leans away from Jimmy and looks on with curiosity.*) Praise Him. Yes, praise the Lord. (*Jimmy looks at Iris and gives her a big bear hug.*) That was a wonderful prayer, Iris. Thank you. The Bible says that whenever you praise the Lord your name is written down on the pages of gold for all to see.

IRIS: He must have a hundred pages with your name on them.

JIMMY: Eso espero!

IRIS: (*she sits back down*). What are you standin' around for? God ain't gonna drain that septic tank. The Bible says those who drain septic tanks for little old ladies will have their name written down on plates of gold for all the angels to see.

JIMMY: Is that so?

BLACKOUT

SCENE II

(Later, the same day. Iris enters from the screen-door. She has her garden gear on; gloves, overalls, wide brim hat, and long boots. She takes off hat and gloves. She sits to pull off boots, but can't really manage them. She gives up and sighs. A young man knocks on the side door. He is about thirty years old, well dressed, carrying a briefcase.)

IRIS: (*does not bother to look up as she has resumed removing her boots*). Is that you, Jimmy? The door is unlocked, come on in. I was just out in the garden. Not much left, you know. Just a few green tomatoes and some beans. Did you mix the rest of the manure into the compost pile? We need to get that done while the rains are still here. (*She finally looks up to see that he has not entered. Thinking the door is locked, she moves to open it.*) Well what are you still standin' out there for? (*She opens the door and realizes it is a stranger.*) We don't want any! (*Turns towards the trailer and shouts.*) Isn't that right, Paul? (*Looks back at man.*) Paul is my big husband. Weighs two hundred and fifty pounds. Six feet five inches tall. Much younger than me. You better leave before he comes out. He hates people—especially sales people. He once bet a vacuum cleaner salesman that there was one thing his machine couldn't suck up. Then he bit his ear off and spit it out on the rug.

SAM: (*unphased, but amused*). I'm not here to sell you anything. May I come in?

IRIS: (*yells towards the trailer*). Is it okay if I let this man onto the porch, Paul? (*After no response.*) He must be in the bathroom, but he'll be out soon enough.

SAM: Are you Mrs. Nellie Brye?

IRIS: Who wants to know?

SAM: I'm a representative of the mining company.

IRIS: Representative? Come on in. What can I do you for?

SAM: Actually, I'm a lawyer. Your husband isn't really in there, is he Mrs. Brye?

IRIS: No. I just do that to scare off the crooks and rapists. And lawyers...but you told me you were a representative. I'd stick with that, if I was you. (*She looks him up and down.*) I don't suppose a sex offender would come knock on the door holdin' a brief case.

SAM: I'm harmless.

IRIS: One of these words just doesn't belong here. See

	if you can pick which one—lawyer and harmless.
SAM:	Well, aren't you delightful. Is your daughter around?
IRIS:	(*sitting*). Margie?
SAM:	A chip off the old block, it seems.
IRIS:	She ain't here. What can I do you for?
SAM:	She told me you were in the hospital.
IRIS:	Amazin' recovery. Hey do you know what a hundred lawyers at the bottom of the ocean is?
SAM:	If Margie isn't here, I can come back later.
IRIS:	A good start! (*She laughs heartily. Sam smiles wryly.*) It was only a joke. Maybe I can help you. Have a seat.
SAM:	The trailer was supposed to be off the property by now. We can't move our equipment in until this all has been scratched. Removal wasn't part of the contract.
IRIS:	The trailer? Why on earth would we want to move the trailer?
SAM:	Didn't your daughter tell you? We bought the land and mineral rights months ago. The lease back agreement is up. Time to go.
IRIS:	(*dismayed*). This can't be! There must be some mistake. (*She stands and walks over to open screen door.*) You go back to your office, young man, and straighten this out. How dare you come here tellin' lies. I want you off this

59

property right now! You go back and talk to your boss. He'll straighten this out. You go back to that office of yours right now.

SAM: I'm sorry, Mrs. Brye. I can't believe you weren't informed about this. But the land is already ours.

IRIS: You seem like a nice young man. Nice suit. Do you have a family? What's your name?

SAM: You can call me Sam. Yes, my wife and I have a little girl.

IRIS: Is your mama still alive?

SAM: Yes, and my father.

IRIS: Is he in good health?

SAM: Well, we are all getting older, aren't we?

IRIS: I pray your mother dies before your father. And may the good Lord see fit to protect your daughter from seein' how this world treats old discarded women who are no longer useful to anyone!

SAM: I really am sorry. But I don't know anything except what's told to me. (*He hands her an envelope from his briefcase.*) You have thirty days.

IRIS: (*she waves off the envelope and walks away*). I'm not Nellie! Nellie is my sister-in-law and she's oblivious to what's happening here. How dare you come and yank the rug out from under a lady that's already layin' in a hospital bed!

SAM: Hey, don't get crotchety with me. Everything we are doing is legal...for a change. Hell, I can't win for losing!

IRIS: Legal? This isn't about the law! It's about compassion. Love for your fellow man. So, you march right back to your office and make this right.

SAM: Can't do that. It's a done deal.

IRIS: Make a lot of money, don't you?

SAM: Yeah, so what. I work my butt off lady. So, don't start preaching your ancient morality crap to me. I'm sick and tired of being blamed for the problems of folks who don't take care of their own affairs. It's not my fault.

IRIS: Well, watch out, Sam. Because when you're eighty, and your body starts to fail, and your mind slips a bit, all that money and your bad attitude ain't gonna do a thing for you.

SAM: When I'm eighty I won't give a shit, lady. Just give me a pill and set me in a chair. You can't stop the inevitable.

IRIS: Oh, you'll care, Sammy baby. You'll care. When your butt starts to rot from pressure sores because the nurses fail to turn your *ass,* you will most definitely care. The pain will be so unbearable that at some point you will lose your mind. You will care then, and you'll wonder why no one else does.

SAM: (*After an awkward pause*). Hey, ma'am, I'm sorry for my language. My wife is having an affair. I've been kind of edgy lately.

IRIS: (*after another awkward pause*). When's the last time you had sex, Sam?

SAM: Excuse me?

IRIS: When was the last time you mounted your wife?

SAM: Long time.

IRIS: Go home, Sam. Light some fancy candles, strip naked and get up on the kitchen table.

SAM: Huh?

IRIS: Lots of floor play, Sam. As soon as your wife walks through the door, start howlin' like a dog. She'll come around.

SAM: (*opens screen door. Looks back at Iris*). Howl? Really?

IRIS: Guaranteed or your money back.

SAM: Couldn't hurt. But the land is still ours. (*He exits.*)

IRIS: Yeah, we'll see about that. (*Iris sits.*) Don't you worry, Patsy. You're not goin' anywhere. (*Pause.*) Oh, Lord, what am I gonna tell Nellie?

JIMMY: (*enters carrying a tire iron*). I heard everything while I was waiting outside. Don't worry, Iris. God will come through. No la dejará sin casa— He won't leave her without a home.

IRIS: God ain't gonna do a damn thing! God does for those who do for themselves. It seems as though Nellie hasn't been doin' a thing to try and solve this problem and now it's too late.

JIMMY: I would not talk that way.

IRIS: What's God gonna do, Jimmy? You are young. I don't expect you to know hardship. Sometimes things happen for the worst with no explanation or hope for better. It's just nature. Survival of the fittest.

JIMMY: God provides for everyone who asks in His name. If you have faith and ask in the Lord's name, you shall receive.

IRIS: Sit down, Jimmy. (*She pauses as she considers what to say.*) When I was a kid, I lived in the backwoods of Arkansas. I spent a lot of time under the trees...alone...I had a favorite waterin' hole I went to every day of every summer that I could sneak away. Not many people knew about it. I always discovered the most curios things in that small pond. One in particular never made any sense to me, until I grew up and had a family of my own.

JIMMY: And what was that?

IRIS: I liked to watch butterflies and turtles. Butterflies are so carefree and gentle. Sometimes I would sit still for hours tryin' to coax a butterfly to land on my hand. Turtles, on the other hand, well, they made me laugh. So slow but very determined. The butterflies never landed on me. They landed on the turtles though. They perched perfectly on their heads. I thought, why on earth would a butterfly want to take a ride on a creature that creeps so slowly along the ground.

JIMMY: (*after a short pause*). To see a different view of the world?

IRIS: I thought it was because they loved one another. At least that was the little fantasy I created in my imagination.

JIMMY: There doesn't have to be a reason.

IRIS: The butterfly drinks the tears of the turtle.

JIMMY: Why?

IRIS: Nature. Turtle tears contain salt. The turtle is slow and unable to swat the butterfly away. The butterfly can safely land and take what they need—just like a scavenger. Nothing graceful about that. Nothing beautiful about the facts. Just nature. (*There is a knock on the door, it is Sam, the lawyer.*) I thought I asked you to leave. You may have claim to this property in thirty days, but for right now, you have no rights here at all.

SAM: (*opening the door*). I have a little problem with my car. The strangest thing. I pulled out of the drive and my two rear tires just fell right off the car.

JIMMY: (*quietly slips the tire iron under the table*).

That can happen out here at this altitude.

SAM: What does the altitude have to do with it?

JIMMY: Does strange things to cars.

SAM: I just need to use your phone, ma'am. If you don't mind.

IRIS: Oh, I'm sorry, we had that disconnected right after you left. Bein' that we're gonna be movin' and all.

SAM: Please? The nearest gas station is at least five miles from here.

JIMMY: Don't worry, the wolves won't come around until the sun sets.

SAM: Wolves?

IRIS: You know, those animals that kill things smaller and weaker than themselves.

SAM: (*angry and somewhat frightened, he slams door and yells as he stomps away*). I'll be back. You can count on that; I will be back!

IRIS: Just like the wolves, Sam. Just like the wolves!

JIMMY: Iris. That wasn't very nice. You should at least let him use the phone.

IRIS: (*retrieves tire iron from under the table*). And what would God think about this?

JIMMY: He was a mean man.

IRIS: Oh, he was just doin' his job.

JIMMY: He should find another. Besides, I'm leaving in a few minutes. I'll help him with the tires.

IRIS: I'm not worried about him. How am I goin' to

tell Nellie?

JIMMY: That's why I came out again. Nellie is not doing so well. She may be in the hospital a little longer than expected.

IRIS: How much longer?

JIMMY: The doctor said at least another week.

IRIS: We have to tell her as soon as possible—before she gets home.

JIMMY: That would be best, I think.

IRIS: (*Iris stands and heads to trailer*). I've got something for you to take to her. (*She exits inside and quickly reenters with a bag.*)

JIMMY: What is that smell?

IRIS: I made some air fresheners. No one likes the odors in a hospital.

JIMMY: (*puts his nose to bag and inhales*). Smells like tobacco.

IRIS: It's skoal. Reminds her of her late husband. He used to dip it. There's some magazines in there too. She likes to cut out the coupons. I threw in the latest stock quotes. I'm still kickin' her patootie.

JIMMY: This is very thoughtful of you. God will bless you, I'm sure. (*He starts to exit but turns back.*) Howling like a dog on the kitchen table?

IRIS: Do you think God's gonna send me to hell?

JIMMY: No, I was wondering how sturdy my kitchen table is.

IRIS: Go on. That lawyer has probably wet his britches by now.

BLACKOUT

SCENE III

(Two weeks later. The sounds of gunshots are heard. Jimmy and Bethany are packing boxes.)

JIMMY: When will the family come to get the rest of her things?

BETH: I'm surprised they aren't here right now, fighting over it all. (*Holding up a box.*) Look at this.

JIMMY: (*walks over to Bethany and reaches into the box. He removes a tiny object.*) It's a table. A little tiny table.

BETH: Nellie used to make miniature houses. Complete with everything. An itsy-bitsy cereal box. An unbelievably detailed antique hutch filled with the most miniscule fine china you have ever seen. Anything you could imagine that would be in a real house.

JIMMY: What about the people?

BETH: That's funny, now that you mention it. She only put people in the bathrooms—on the toilets. Weird, Huh?

JIMMY: Nellie was a very special person.

BETH: I remember how Vern, her husband, would come in from the fields with four or five Mexican men, Nellie would feed all of them and never say a word. She could barely afford to feed her kids. Nellie could always make a meal stretch. I wish I would have asked her how she managed to send all those men home on full stomachs. All the Mexicans adored Nellie and Vern.

JIMMY: Those men at the funeral...were those some of the men that...

BETH: Yes, most of them can't speak much English.

JIMMY: They were all crying. Did you see. I've never seen so many grown men cry. She will be missed.

BETH: (*almost to tears*). Yeah, she sure will. (*Another gunshot rings out.*) Jimmy, would you go check on my mother? What on earth is she shooting at?

JIMMY: She is okay. Just shooting into a dirt bank.

BETH: Nellie was Mom's last friend.

JIMMY: She will make more.

BETH: No. You don't understand. Nellie was Mom's *last* friend. No one else living comes from the same place as my mom. Mom is from a time and a place that hasn't existed in for many decades. Nellie knew it well. They could relate.

JIMMY: She will be okay. That Iris est loca en la cabeza.

BETH: Loca means crazy, Right? (*Jimmy nods.*) Yeah, you know my mom.

JIMMY: Iris has a lot of pride. By the way, I don't think

she has found a place to live yet.

BETH: I know. She makes me so angry. She could have put her name on a waiting list for low income housing months ago. I wish she could live with my husband and me, but...

JIMMY: But what?

BETH: Mom and I don't talk.

JIMMY: Isn't that good? You don't talk; you don't fight.

BETH: Sometimes conflict is greatest during silence. I need to forgive my mom for a lot of things, but she makes it pretty difficult.

JIMMY: You don't need Iris's cooperation to forgive her.

BETH: Yes, I do.

JIMMY: No, really, you don't. I don't know what happened between you but whatever it was— you must forgive her.

BETH: Excuse me, Jimmy, but I think you are a bit... well, naïve. And in this case, you really don't have any idea what you're talking about. So...

JIMMY: I know enough to see that you are hurting for something that happened a long time ago. Have you ever read about or studied the life and death of Jesus Christ? A lot of people have come to understand that Jesus is the actual Creator God, and if that's true, He has a lot of powerful things to say on the subject of forgiveness. Maybe you need to figure out who

Jesus is, and trust Him about what he had to say.

BETH: My mom is a selfish, hard woman. Not a mother at all. Mothers are supposed to be soft, like down feathers, warm like a blanket on a cold winter's night. Like...Nellie. (*Pause.*) I have tried. God knows, I've tried to love that woman. I honestly don't know if I do. Do you have any idea how much that hurts—to say you don't love the woman that brought you life? It affects every single thing I do. Every decision I make. Every person I meet. So, don't stand there with your holier than thou attitude and tell me how I should feel about my mom. I would have been better off if she had died instead of my father. At least then I could have created an imaginary memory of her that I could live with!

JIMMY: My mom died when I was five. I hated her so much for that—for most of my life.

BETH: How can you hate someone for something that wasn't their fault?

JIMMY: She overdosed on some drug. She was an addict. But I loved her, until I hated her. Hate is easy, it has no requirements.

BETH: I don't know if I even want to forgive her anymore.

JIMMY: That's why you are here, no? After Nellie's

death? You don't have much time left to decide.

BETH: I don't know where to start.

JIMMY: There is a saying in my family: Forgiveness is the most selfish act one can commit that gives so much to others.

BETH: You just made that up.

JIMMY: Yeah. Pretty good, huh?

BETH: I wish I could have gotten to know you better. (*Iris enters through the side door, shotgun in hand.*) Run out of shells, Mom?

IRIS: No. Ran out of targets!

BETH: Targets? What were you shooting at?

IRIS: Mosquitoes! Damn things are as thick as the hair on a dog's back! And big! What are you two a doin'?

BETH: I thought I would try and organize a few things before I leave tomorrow.

IRIS: I hope Marg doesn't see you doin' that. She might accuse you of stealin'.

BETH: I can deal with Margie.

IRIS: (*Turns to Jimmy*). And you! What are you a doin'?

JIMMY: What? What am I doing? I come to help you, no? You no want my help? Fine! I no give you my help. I drive my truck here, waste my gasoline. Gas not cheap, you know? So, what do I get? I leave my family to come help you

72

and what do you do? You ask me what am I doing? A hora si nomas esto me faltaba vengo aqui a ayudarle a est vieja me sale con, what am I doing? O hala que dios le ensene la luz porque como va a ahortia va directo al infierno con Margie! (*Iris and Bethany exchange looks.*)

IRIS: (*to Bethany*). He's bilingual, you know. What do I need, Jimmy? There's nothing left to do here. Nellie's kids are comin' tomorrow to clear it out. Thick as thieves they are. Jimmy?

JIMMY: Yes?

IRIS: Have you ever seen flies buzz around a cow's butt?

JIMMY: Well, yes...

IRIS: That's what it'll look like around here tomorrow. They'll get every last dried up crumb! Just like the flies on a cow's butt!

BETH: Mom!

IRIS: It's true.

BETH: It's theirs to take.

IRIS: Do you think so, Jimmy? That it's theirs to take?

JIMMY: I don't know.

IRIS: What does God have to say on the subject?

JIMMY: No estoy seguro.

IRIS: Hmph! Finally, something he doesn't know. (*Iris exits into trailer.*)

JIMMY: It's time for me to go. Good luck with that one. (*He nods in Iris's direction.*)

BETH: Thanks again, Jimmy. I can't tell you how much we appreciated what you did for Nellie. She thought the world of you. You brought her an armful of peace.

JIMMY: I was just doing my job, señora.

BETH: You went way beyond what you were paid to do.

JIMMY: I never had a mama, remember? (*Jimmy opens side door to exit as Iris enters form trailer.*)

IRIS: Well, hold your horses. (*She walks over to Jimmy and hands him a brown paper bag.*) Here, Nellie would have wanted you to have this.

JIMMY: (*looks inside*). I cannot take all of this.

IRIS: Nellie knew about your trips over the border.

JIMMY: What are you talking about?

IRIS: Those Mexican friends that Nellie had, they told us about your work with the homeless kids.

JIMMY: Must be some other Jimmy.

IRIS: Lechuga cabeza! Just take it and do with it as you see fit. She's been sockin' it away for you ever since she found out. None of Nellie's kids know anything about this. They would just kill one another tryin' to get at it. You would be

74

doin' them a favor. (*He still seems hesitant to take it.*) She wanted it to go to the kids. Take it.

JIMMY: (*reluctantly agrees*). You know, there's just one thing I cannot understand with you Americans. You are very nice and generous. You give more than any other people, but...

BETH: But what?

JIMMY: Why can't families live together? Stay together? Why do you live so far apart? Where I was born, many generations live in the same house. It's expected.

IRIS: Where you're from, people can't afford to live anywhere but together.

JIMMY: (*shrugs in acknowledgement. Holds up bag*). Thanks. This will go to good use.

IRIS: I know it will.

JIMMY: God bless. (*He exits.*)

BETH: God bless you too, Jimmy. (*She turns to Iris.*) I cleaned out the refrigerator.

IRIS: That's nice. (*Iris attends to the rabbit hutch.*)

BETH: I packed up all the dry goods that were in the kitchen cabinets. I thought you might want to take them with you.

IRIS: With me? Where?

BETH: I hate how you do this to me, Mom. I'll stay a few more days and help you find another apartment. If there's anything of yours here, let me know and we can put it in the truck.

IRIS: Nothing here is mine. I don't want Margie
          talkin' about me for the next ten years. Tellin'
          everyone what a big thief I am.

BETH: Quit worrying about Margie.

IRIS: She's an evil woman. I've never seen anyone so
          evil in all my days. To do what she did to her
          mother. Her own mother.

BETH: She was just trying to do what was best. It's not
          easy, you know.

IRIS: Ha! What was best for *Marg*! Marg is like a
          fruit worm. She gets into the most sensitive
          places and just starts eatin' her way
          through...all the way to the core. Whatever she
          doesn't consume, she leaves to rot.

BETH: That's a bit severe. No one deserves to be
          talked about like that, Mom.

IRIS: She kept wormin' her way in here. Sometimes I
          thank God he took Nellie when he did. Better
          to die of heart failure than of a broken heart.
          Marg would have taken this place away from
          Nellie one way or another.

BETH: I'm sure Margie would have postponed the
          transfer of the land if she had known how ill
          Nellie was.

IRIS: Don't be so sure. Nellie was not ready to die,
          Beth. The thought of losing her home pushed
          her over the edge. Marg is a resentful little
          worm, Beth. Don't kid yourself.

BETH: Do you know something you're not telling me?

IRIS: (*short pause*). What? What do I know? Only
         what I see. Nothing you can't see for yourself.
         (*Margie enters from side door.*)

MARG: Anybody got an apple? I'm starving. Nice to
         see you again, Beth. I noticed you brought that
         big pick-up truck of yours.

IRIS: Don't worry, Margie. It's leaving just as empty
         as it came.

MARG: Well of course it is. I hardly think Bethany
         would steal from her own cousins. Just makes
         me wonder why she didn't drive her car, that's
         all. (*She begins inspecting the place, looking in
         boxes.*) It's a shame none of your kids have
         room for you, Iris. I was working on a way to
         have Mom come live at my house. I had just
         asked George about adding an addition onto
         the house. He was actually starting to make
         plans and then Mom up and kicked the bucket.

BETH: She probably heard you were going to ask her
         to move it with you. (*Iris conceals a laugh.*)

MARG: What is that supposed to mean?

BETH: Nothing, Margie. That was really nice of you.
         Nellie would have been pleased. Would you
         like a drink? I packed the vodka, but I can dig
         it out.

MARG: Packed the vodka? What in the hell for? Where
         you going with the vodka? I guess I'll have to

keep an eye on you two.

BETH: Oh, give me a break, Margie. I was just trying to help you out.

MARG: Well of course you were, sugar. Now just go right back in the house and unpack everything.

BETH: Unpack? Why?

MARG: I just want to be able to make a little inventory, that's all. It's hard to see everything when it's all packed away in boxes.

BETH: I only packed the kitchen stuff. Canned goods and some knickknacks.

MARG: It's up to me to make sure all my brothers and sisters get their fair share of things and I can hardly do that when everything's in boxes already. You're a dear for trying to help, but I wish you wouldn't, unless I were to ask, of course. You understand, don't you, honey?

BETH: Yes, quite clear.

MARG: I've done it again, haven't I? Please forgive me, Beth, but my mom did just pass away and I'm a little upset. That's all. Sometimes I say things I shouldn't.

IRIS: Yeah? Well, what was your excuse when Nellie was alive?

BETH: Mom!

MARG: That's okay, Beth. Your mom is just old and feeble. She doesn't have any manners left anymore.

IRIS: You old worm! You're nothing but an old grub! Don't you think for one minute that I'm too old to know what's goin' on around here.

MARG: Around here? Let's remember that you haven't got a lot of say around here anymore, Iris. And if you continue to insult me, I'm going to have to ask you to leave. (*She picks up a half-eaten banana off the table.*) Is anyone going to eat the rest of this banana?

BETH: There's a whole one on top of the fridge.

MARG: This will be just fine, thanks. (*She heads up steps towards trailer door.*) Beth, will you help me take some boxes to the car. I packed a few the other day and I want to start making a little room to move around.

IRIS: I thought you wanted to wait so all the kids could come over and look through the stuff together?

MARG: These boxes are nothing. Just garbage, really. Cone on, Beth, they're pretty heavy. (*Bethany lifts an eyebrow and shrugs as they both exit into the trailer.*)

IRIS: (*sarcastically, loud enough for Margie to hear her from inside the trailer*). I'll just start unpacking these boxes, Marg, so you can get a good look-see.

MARG: (*sticks her head out of the door*). No, no, that won't be necessary. I mean, since you already made the mistake of packing them, we may as well just leave it. (*Margie opens the door wider for Bethany, who is carrying a box. She follows with her own box.*) Careful, Beth.

BETH: These are awful heavy. What's in them?

MARG: Oh, just some old books that Mom had.

IRIS: I never heard books clank like antique china.

MARG: Mom would have wanted me to have these. Besides, my sister already has a nice set of...books. (*They set the boxes on the table.*)

IRIS: I won't say anything. But Carol is going to know the china is missing.

MARG: I'll make something up.

IRIS: Marg, you know how much I cared about your mother. She was like a sister to me.

MARG: What do you want, Iris?

IRIS: Why don't I go get you a little drink. (*Iris quickly exits into trailer. She speaks through kitchen window.*) You just sit and rest a spell, Marg. Take a break.

MARG: (*to Bethany*). She must want some of Maw's Jewelry.

BETH: I Hardly think she would ask for jewelry.

BETH: People get greedy when someone dies. It's sad but I've seen it happen time and time again.

BETH: Have you?

IRIS: (*enters with a drink for Margie and a pitcher of tea for herself and Bethany. Bethany takes* the pitcher form her and sets it on the table). I will understand if you say no. But I kind of wanted to have something of Nellie's to take with me.

MARG: (*under her breath to Bethany*). Here goes. (*Looks up at Iris.*) Anything in particular?

IRIS: Patsy and I have become real close. And Patsy's personality is a lot like Nellie's. I wouldn't even need to take the cage. I can make a new one. Patsy has always been real good company. I'd be willing to give you a little money for her, if you like.

MARG: (*obviously uncomfortable and at a momentary loss for words*). I'm sorry, but I just took that rabbit down to the veterinarian. She was so old. The vet didn't think we could find a home for her so I had her put to sleep. (*She lights a cigarette.*) I'm sorry. I didn't know she meant that much to you. Let alone that you would have a way to keep her. You should have mentioned something earlier.

IRIS: (*Iris appears confused. She stands and wanders around absentmindedly*). She's gone? Patsy is gone? I thought you had taken her home with you. She was such a sweet little girl. If you two will excuse me, I think I'll get some fresh air. (*She opens screen door and exits.*)

BETH: (*waits until her mother is out of earshot*). How could you? You knew how much Mom loved that rabbit.

MARG: No, I didn't. She cooked the other one!

BETH: According to you.

MARG: Oh, it just so happened to disappear on the day we had rabbit stew?

BETH: You are evil. I had no idea how bad the years had been to you.

MARG: Yes, Saint Bethany. Allow me to bow down before Saint Bethany and ask for forgiveness. Look, you and I are no different!

BETH: I could never do some of the things you pull.

MARG: Did you see the place where your mom was living before she came back here? What a roach pit that was. I can guarantee you this, I would have died before I let my mom move into that poverty-stricken, rat-infested dump.

BETH: How dare you blame that on me. My mom insists on living on her own. She wants to remain independent.

MARG: Is that what you tell yourself before you go to bed at night? Does that help you get to sleep while mice are gnawing through your mother's bag of government flour that she paid for with her government handouts?

BETH: How dare you. I've tried to do everything I possibly could for her. I have been the best

	daughter I could.
MARG:	No, you haven't. Everyone knows how much resentment you have towards her. We all know about your relationship with your step-father and why Iris sent you to live with us and later to an orphanage. Everyone knows, Bethany.
BETH:	You don't know anything. And you're the one who has gotten fat!
MARG:	Step-daddy's little girl. It wasn't your fault. It was Iris's fault. She knew what he was doing to her little girl, but she just let it continue. As long as it kept her man happy, she just turned and looked the other way.
BETH:	Shut-up you wretched bitch! Shut your mouth or I'll...
MARG:	Or you'll what? Oh, quit feeling sorry for yourself. That all happened a long time ago. We have all had a hard life and I'm fed up with everyone feeling sorry for sweet little Bethany. Pretty little Bethany! How was it making love to Daddy? I bet Bethany wasn't so sweet then.
BETH:	(*picks up shotgun left by Iris and points it at Margie. She seems calm and collected*). Mom was right, you are evil. I should put you out of your misery.
MARG:	(*neither the gun or Bethany's resolve phases Margie*). Get that gun out of my face! (*Iris enters but says nothing.*) I'm just trying to

help you. I know it's her fault. (*She nods towards Iris.*) That's who you should be pointing a gun at. She never loved you. She said herself that she shouldn't have had a girl. I heard her say that to Mom. She's the reason for your pain. She knew what that man was doing to you. (*Margie turns towards Iris.*) Why didn't you stop him, Iris? Why didn't you take that shotgun and end it? Wasn't your little girl worth it? What kind of mother are you?

BETH: Go to hell!

IRIS: Give me the gun. (*After no response, she moves closer to Bethany.*) I'm a much better shot than you are. (*Iris slowly removes the gun from Bethany's hands.*)

BETH: (*fighting back tears*). Didn't you love me, Mom? Why did you let him do those things to me? I was just a little girl. I always thought you would come to my rescue because that's what moms do, right? But you never came. Night after night. You never came. And then you sent me away. You sent *me* away. I felt so guilty. I thought I had done something wrong. But I didn't do anything wrong, Mom. It wasn't my fault.

IRIS: There is no reason for what happened to you. I didn't know about it until it was much too late. I did the only thing I knew how to do. I divorced him and I tried to find you a better home.

BETH: An orphanage?

IRIS: It was only supposed to have been temporary—for a few months. Until I could get back up on my feet. I was a single mother with no money, no help. I was lost. I always loved you, Bethany. But all that was a long time ago and I'm too old and tired to change the past.

MARG: And you thought I was evil. She won't even try to make up for all the crap she put you through.

IRIS: I had little control over the things that happened to Bethany and me. But you, you have had complete control over what has happened here the last few months.

MARG: What are you trying to say?

IRIS: You killed your mother. You may not have pointed a gun in her face, but you were responsible for her death.

BETH: Mom, please, don't...

MARG: It's okay. I want to hear what she has to say.

IRIS: I happen to know that you could only exercise power of attorney if Nellie was ill. So, you waited until she was in the hospital and you made your move. Just like a rattler—quick, concise, and deadly.

BETH: Why did you do all this while Nellie was sick?

Couldn't you have postponed it for a while, even a month?

MARG: I did not cause Mom's death. Her heart has been weak for many years.

IRIS: No, I suppose you didn't realize that losing her home would kill her. You may not have known it would stop her heart from beating, but it did.

MARG: Listen to this, Beth. She can't muster up the strength to apologize to you, but she sure as hell can accuse me of murder.

IRIS: Nursing homes are very expensive, aren't they, Margie? Much more costly than a memorial service.

MARG: (*Margie is becoming more and more incensed*). Get out of here, you resentful old woman! Even with our problems, she was still my mother. How can you say these things to me so soon after her death? No one, not even me, deserves this.

IRIS: I got a call from her bank, yesterday. It seems as though you had been doing a little research to find out if Nellie had any investments—stock investments.

BETH: Mom, this is really none of our business. Perhaps we should go.

IRIS: She wasn't even cold yet, Marg.

BETH: I don't get it. You won't even consider discussing our problems—your own daughter.

But bring on the rest of the world's concerns and you're the first to get in line.

IRIS: I owe it to Nellie!

BETH: Fine! You two duke it out. I'm leaving. You should think about cleaning out your own closets first, Mom.

(*She exits, but remains close to the door, listening.*)

MARG: (*ignores Bethany and moves in front of Iris*). I happen to know Mom was heavily invested in the stock market, but it wasn't in her will.

IRIS: (*laughs*). Your mom didn't own any stock.

MARG: That's not true. She had thousands invested.

IRIS: Where do you think she would have gotten that kind of money to chance on stocks?

MARG: If she didn't own any stock then why were you two always talking about it? And I saw plenty of notes on her transactions.

IRIS: It was a game. A what if...

MARG: What are you talking about?

IRIS: She and I played an imaginary stock market...with imaginary money. It was a friendly game and I admit, sometimes we got a little competitive...but it wasn't real.

MARG: You mean she doesn't have anything? Nothing? But I was planning to...I...I can't believe this. I thought Mom had lots of money. There must be money somewhere? Maybe she kept it hid out in her garden. There's got to be more money somewhere! By the time we divide up the money from the sale of this lousy piece of land, there's hardly anything...

IRIS: You be honest with me, Margie, and I'll tell you exactly what Nellie did with her meager savings.

MARG: Why are you doing this to me?

IRIS: This is the way Nellie wanted it. She thought that in order for you to be forgiven, you would have to admit to another living person the exact nature of your wrongs.

MARG: Does anyone else know about the money? (*Iris shakes her head.*) Yes, I wanted the money from the sale of the land. The mines aren't as profitable as what they used to be. The offers were getting lower and lower. As it is, we only got half of what was offered two years ago. My dad worked hard for this land and we deserved to get the most out of it. Mom was very selfish. And she was also much sicker than she ever let on. The doctors only gave her a few months...and that was over a year ago.

IRIS: You could have waited.

MARG: No. The last offer had to be signed. I waited until the last possible moment.

IRIS: You needed power of attorney and you couldn't get that until she was admitted into the

	hospital. You knew that all of this stress would kill her.
MARG:	Is that what you want to believe? Does it make you feel like you're not the only evil person in the family? I didn't exactly enjoy this, ya' know.
IRIS:	Nellie was right. Your tears are slow to fall. But they will fall one day, and I hope you'll be prepared, because the dam is going to overflow.
BETH:	(*entering*). Mom, didn't you once tell me that Nellie stored her money in coffee cans because she didn't trust the banks? (*She winks at Iris.*)
IRIS:	Well...
BETH:	And wasn't Nellie spending a lot of time in the garden before she went into the hospital?
IRIS:	Yes. Now that you mention it, that's right when all those coffee cans stated disappearin'. (*Before Iris can get another word out, Margie grabs a shovel from the corner of the porch and exits towards the garden.*) Too bad I didn't think of this before. It would have saved me from havin' to till the soil. (*Looks out towards garden.*) Wow! Look at that dirt fly!
BETH:	Mom, did you know?
IRIS:	Marg left a trail a mile long. She has five siblings to split the money received for the land. That wasn't enough to wet her appetite.

BETH: Forget about Margie. She lost her chance.
          (*Pauses.*) Did you know what he did to me?

IRIS: Don't you already know the answer?

BETH: I want to hear you say it.

IRIS: Some part of me knew. Yes. (*Both stand in
          silence for a long moment.*) I'm glad you went
          to one of those therapists. Is he good?

BETH: I think she saved my life. I'm okay now. I
          mean, I'm still healing, but...things are going
          to be okay...eventually. I have hope.

IRIS: Can you ever forgive me?

BETH: Perhaps. (*After no response from Iris.*) Guess I
          had better get going.

IRIS: Sure.

BETH: Before the sun sets.

IRIS: Yes.

BETH: I put some books in your car.

IRIS: That's nice.

BETH: John Grisham and a couple of westerns.

IRIS: My favorites.

BETH: Lonesome Dove.

IRIS: Take good care, Beth.

BETH: You too, Mom.

IRIS: Write.

BETH: (*handing her mom an envelope*). Here's a little
          money. If you need anything else...

IRIS: I'll call. (*Bethany exits only to re-enter a few
          moments later.*)

BETH: (*out of duty, not convinced*). Mom, come stay with Dominick and me until we find you a place to live.

IRIS: (*stunned, but trying not to show it*). What would I do with my things?

BETH: We can put them in storage.

IRIS: Storage? My life in storage? I'll feel like a perpetual visitor.

BETH: It is just temporary. And we can keep out whatever you will need for the next couple of months.

IRIS: No, I don't want to be a burden.

BETH: You won't be, Mom. (*Iris looks truly touched and a sense of relief has overcome her. It is the most vulnerable Bethany has ever seen her. Bethany gently wraps her mother in a loving embrace. The two awkwardly hold one another for a few seconds.*) I don't think you have ever asked me for a hug.

IRIS: I'm sorry.

BETH: I think you're getting soft in your old age.

IRIS: How would you know if we haven't been huggin'?

BETH: Do you remember the story about the butterfly and the turtle?

IRIS: You couldn't have been more than five years old when I told you that story.

BETH: I think about it a lot. The sickly butterfly that

drank the magic tears of the turtle so she could fly back to her family and live happily ever after.

IRIS: That's not the way I told it.

BETH: That's the way I remember it. The butterfly got separated from her family and became very ill. One day when the butterfly had no strength left, she glided down to the forest floor to die.

IRIS: And a turtle saw the butterfly take her last breath. The turtle was so saddened by seeing the butterfly lying on the ground all by herself that he cried many tears.

BETH: The turtle tears fell on the butterfly and she magically fluttered her wings. But they weren't the same brown wings, they were brilliant blue. The butterfly and turtle became the best of friends until she fell in love and had a new family all her own. But even to this day butterflies all over the world light on turtles and drink their tears. (*Pauses.*) When I was in the orphanage, I used to steal the other kid's tears. I thought if turtles could have magic tears, surely kids could too. So, I wiped their tears away with my hand. I knew those magic tears would bring me back home. Tell me the story, Mom. The way you used to. About the magic turtle tears.

IRIS: A thousand years ago there was a dark forest

chock-full of towering trees, giant ferns, colorful birds, fluttering butterflies, and pudgy round turtles... (*A tear rolls down Bethany's cheek and Iris wipes it away with her hand.*)

BETH: Come home with me, Mom.

IRIS: Beth, please forgive me. (*She takes Bethany's head in her hands.*) I'm so sorry.

BETH: After all of these years, who would have thought, there is still magic in turtle tears.

LIGHTS FADE

THE END

Peggy Cozzi (Nellie) and Bette Rae (Iris)

Original Production Still

Other Books and Plays by J. Suthern Hicks:
Where the Garden Begins (Messengers and Thieves, Book 1)
A Leaf of Faith (Messengers and Thieves, Book 2)
Home, Hearth, and Oreos: A One Act Play
Charlie and Chocolate's Purrfect Prayer
Charlie and Chocolate's Furry Forgiveness

www.ingramcontent.com/pod-product-compliance
Lightning Source LLC
Chambersburg PA
CBHW021134020426
42331CB00005B/767